NATIVE AMERICAN HEROES

OSCEOLA, TECUMSEH & COCHISE

by Ann McGovern

SCHOLASTIC INC.

PHOTO CREDITS: Front and back cover: Jim Madsen for Scholastic; vii: Jim Madsen for Scholastic; viii: George Catlin/Library of Congress; p2: Charles Bird King/Library of Congress; p7: The New York Public Library/Art Resource; p8: North Wind Picture Archives; p13: The Granger Collection; p16: Jim McMahon for Scholastic; p22: T.F. Gray and James, 1837/Library of Congress; p25: North Wind Picture Archives; p29: T.F. Gray and James, 1837/Library of Congress; p34: The Granger Collection; p36: George Catlin/Library of Congress; p38: National Park Service; p39: Post and Courier and AP/YGS Group; p41: Jim Madsen for Scholastic; p42: North Wind Picture Archives; p45: NativeStock Pictures; p47: North Wind Picture Archives; p50: North Wind Picture Archives; p54: Library of Congress; p56: North Wind Picture Archives; p59: Jim McMahon for Scholastic; p63: North Wind Picture Archives/The Image Works; p67: Library of Congress; p68: Bettmann/Corbis; p73: Detroit Historical Society; p77: Library of Congress; p83: Jim Madsen for Scholastic; p84: The Granger Collection; p86: Library of Congress; p89: The Granger Collection; p90—91: Jim McMahon for Scholastic; p96: Corbis; p101: North Wind Picture Archives; p105: National Archives; p112: Look and Learn/Bridgeman Art Library; p115: Library of Congress; p119: Library of Congress.

Library of Congress Cataloging-in-Publication Data
McGovern, Ann.
Native American heroes / by Ann McGovern ; cover illustration by Jim Madsen.
p. cm.

ISBN 978-0-545-46720-9

1. Indians of North America—Kings and rulers—Biography—Juvenile literature.
2. Heroes—Juvenile literature. I. Madsen, Jim, 1964- II. Title.

E89.M37 2013
973.04'9700922—dc23
2013006133

12 11 10 9 8 7 6 5   16 17 18/0

Printed in the U.S.A.   40
This edition first printing, November 2013

Book design by Kay Petronio

CONTENTS

HOW TO SAY THESE NATIVE AMERICAN NAMES

Algonquian (tribal Nation or language)	**Al-GON-kwee-in**
Aravaipa (an Apache tribe)	**Ah-rah-VI-pa**
Apache (tribal Nation or language)	**Uh-PATCH-ee**
Chiricahua (Apache tribe to which Cochise belonged)	**Chir-ic-KOW-wa**
Cochise (Apache chief)	**Co-CHEEZ**
Coyotero (an Apache tribe)	**Kī-oh-TARE-oh**
Laulewasika (Tecumseh's youngest brother)	**Law-lee-WA-sick-ah**
Micanopy (head chief of the Seminoles)	**Mi-kun-NO-pea**
Osceola (Seminole leader)	**Ah-see-OH-la**
Seminole (tribal Nation or language)	**SEM-in-ole**
Shawnee (tribal Nation or language)	**Shaw-NEE**
Tecumseh (Shawnee chief)	**Teh-KUM-seh**

ative American Heroes tells the exciting and tragic stories of three great Native American leaders who fought bravely for their people's freedom and their right to live on their own lands. The battles took place in the Florida swamps, in the Midwest, and on the Western Plains, at a time when the United States was expanding rapidly. Lands were seized and thousands of people were killed or taken captive in the name of progress.

Please note that there may appear to be spelling, capitalization, and/or grammatical errors in several quotes in this book. These instances were retained to match the original texts. Also, since certain events may not have been documented at the time they happened, some information about these heroes' lives may be known only from legends or anecdotes. The author calls out such information by introducing it using phrases like "according to legend," "it is said," or "many believe."

These Native American heroes' stories are a part of the long struggle for human liberty in the United States — as well as tragic chapters in the history of the first Americans.

OSCEOLA

Osceola.
A painting
by George
Catlin.

"SEIZE HIM!"

A Seminole named Osceola kept his dark eyes on the face of General Wiley Thompson.

The general was speaking — earnestly, a little impatiently — to the Seminole leaders he had called together.

He was saying, "Fine fertile lands await you in the western country. Good hunting grounds you can keep forever. The United States will give you seeds, tools, money."

The Seminoles had heard these words before. They were words of promise. Treaty words. Thompson called this council in 1834 to enforce the terms of two treaties that the Seminoles had already signed. These treaties would send them from their Florida homeland forever. The United States government wanted the Seminoles to move from Florida to the West.

Osceola was present at this council. He was not a chief, not even a lesser chief. Yet the principal chief

Micanopy. Principal Chief of the Seminoles.

of the Florida Seminoles, Micanopy, looked to him as a leader.

Osceola, too, had heard Thompson's promises before. And now his thoughts were bitter. *The white man wants our groves of orange trees, our fine harbors, our full forests, and warm fertile lands. But they are ours. Here are our fish and birds and animals, the graves of our fathers, the grounds of our children.*

Legend has it that at one treaty signing, Osceola had walked boldly to the table where the treaty lay awaiting signatures. Eagerly, the white man had pushed the quill pen toward him. Osceola did not look at it. Instead, he drew out his hunting knife. Then he plunged the knife into the treaty paper, pinning it to the rough pine table. "This," he said, "is the only treaty I make with the whites."

And at this council in 1834, Osceola still did not intend to agree to any terms set forth by the white man. Thompson ordered him to acknowledge the former treaties, but Osceola refused. It took four soldiers to subdue Osceola. They put him in irons and threw him into prison.

Osceola was told that he would be released — but not until he agreed to the terms of the treaties.

2

A TERRIBLE TREATY

ocked in the dark prison, Osceola's thoughts were bitter.

He knew these were terrible treaties. He could not respect them. It was not only Seminole land that the white men wanted. They wanted the Seminoles whose skins were black. For the treaty said that no Seminole who had the blood of the black man could go to the western country.

How this would tear brother from brother! Wife would be taken from husband. Child would be torn from parents. For among the Seminoles the black man and the native people had lived together now for a long, long time. The blood of many of them ran together through the children of many marriages.

Some of the blacks among the Seminoles had been born free. Others had run away from slavery on plantations in the United States. They had fled to the forests and swamps of Florida. There, the runaways had settled among the free blacks and in the Seminole villages.

The Seminoles befriended the runaways. They taught the blacks how to carve cypress canoes and how to make bread from the coontie plant. The blacks taught the Seminoles better ways of farming.

Now who could tell if a black man had been born free, or had bought his freedom from a white man, or if he was the grandson of a Seminole chief? And what did it matter? Through the years, the black men and the native people had become part of one tribe, one Seminole Nation.

But the slave catchers never gave up. No Seminole was really safe. In treaty after treaty the Seminoles had been promised that *this time* white men would not be allowed to hunt or settle or intrude upon their land. Still, the Seminole borders were crossed. Villages were raided, cattle were stolen, crops were destroyed. And Black Seminoles were seized as slaves.

In 1817, what is now known as the First Seminole War started when an American general sent his men across the Spanish border into Florida to arrest a Seminole chief accused of sheltering escaped slaves. Americans living in the southeast had long wanted the U.S. to take the Florida territory from Spain. The First Seminole War gave them the opportunity to do just that, and by February 1819, it was done. The war was over; Spain had been defeated. Florida now belonged to the U.S.

And ever since then, the whites had been pressing harder and harder. Get the Seminoles out to the West! The whites did not, however, want the Black Seminoles to leave Florida. They would be worth a fortune to them as slaves.

Now Thompson was asking Osceola to respect the treaties that would send the Seminoles from their homeland and deliver his black brothers into the hands of the slave owners.

How could he agree to such treaties?!

But only if he agreed to respect the terms of the signed treaties would he be released from prison.

Very well, thought Osceola. *I will use the white man's trickery. I will agree to respect this white man's treaties so I can leave his prison. But I will never really give up our land or betray our brothers.*

Osceola was released from prison. He had told Thompson that he would come back with other opposing chiefs, who would then also acknowledge the treaties.

3

OSCEOLA LEARNS

sceola did not talk lightly of war or of killing. He never forgot what his mother had taught him: *Do not take a life unless your own is in danger.*

He knew, too, what war would mean for his people, the suffering it would bring. In wartime they would have to leave their *chickees* — their thatched log houses — to live in the marshy, murky swamps.

They could not build their eating houses, where there was always a *sofkee* kettle bubbling with a turtle steak or a juicy venison or fish stew. In wartime whatever fish they could catch they would eat raw.

And no longer would his people be able to sit gazing for hours into a fire smelling of the rich pitch pine. In wartime there must be no fires for the enemy to see.

Osceola knew well the hardships of war, for he had spent much of his childhood in such a time.

A Seminole chickee. Because of the warm climate, the house is open on all sides. The floor is raised from the muddy ground. And the roof, made of thatched palmetto leaves, makes an umbrella against sun and rain.

War had forced Osceola and his mother to flee the land of Alabama, where, in approximately 1804, Osceola was born. When he was a child, he and his mother moved to Spanish Florida. There they were taken prisoners during the First Seminole War. When they were freed, they settled in a Seminole village in central Florida.

In his Florida home, Osceola learned early how to live as a wanderer. He learned to move swiftly and with grace. From the time he was a boy, the other Seminoles called him a bold hunter and a fine fisherman. His bright arrows always found their mark. And few could spear so well the small silver fish in the lake.

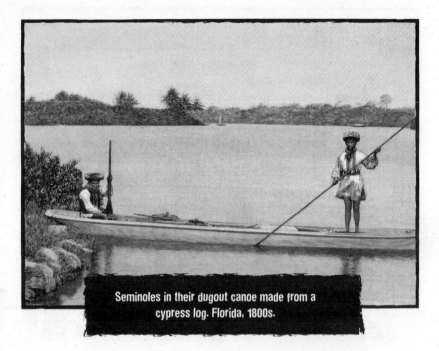

Seminoles in their dugout canoe made from a cypress log. Florida, 1800s.

Osceola learned the names of plants and creatures. He learned which berries and nuts and fruits could be eaten and which ones were poisonous. He learned how to make a cup from a leaf to drink the clear Florida water.

Osceola learned to endure hardship. He grew used to the cold nights, the biting mosquitoes, and the cries of wild animals.

He grew to manhood without fear. He grew to manhood as a Seminole.

Now, as a man, what Osceola could not grow used to was the way white men felt about his native people. To Osceola it seemed that most white men looked upon the

Seminoles as creatures without human feelings — to be tricked, to be cheated, to be destroyed.

Now a white man, Thompson, was asking him, Osceola, to betray his people.

They want me to respect their treaties, he thought. *Very well, let the Seminole learn to lie as the white man lies.*

Osceola had agreed to respect the treaties. For he needed to be free in the days ahead.

Free to fight.

4
"THE SPIRIT OF WAR"

ixteen chiefs and sub-chiefs also agreed to acknowledge the treaty. "It is no use trying to fight the mighty forces of the white man," they said. "We must prepare to leave our homes."

General Wiley Thompson ordered the Seminole chiefs to bring their people to Tampa Bay, Florida, by 1835, the following year. The Seminole Indians would be taken from there to the West.

Osceola did not intend to give up the land. And he tried again and again to strengthen the will of the other leaders. Osceola knew that the Seminole Nation was weak in number — there were only about fifteen hundred Seminole warriors compared to many thousand white soldiers. But he believed his nation was strong. They knew things that the white men did not know about how to survive in swamps, where this war would be fought. Osceola was convinced they should fight.

Those chiefs who had agreed to leave were nevertheless fearful. For one thing, they were afraid of old enemy tribes awaiting them in the West.

They appealed to Thompson for special protection in their new home. Thompson sent their request to the U.S. government in Washington, DC. The answer came back a few weeks later. Their wish would not be granted.

Osceola saw this as more proof that the white men would never help his people. He begged Micanopy, the principal chief, to call a council of war. This Micanopy did.

Osceola's words at the council gave strength to some of the weak, but they struck fear into those who would still go west. Osceola spoke of the importance of saving their homes and their land. But, like the U.S. government, he, too, issued threats to his people. He threatened that if any of the Seminoles sold their land or property to the whites, then he would consider them traitors. The punishment for treason would be death.

Frightened by Osceola's threats, five of the chiefs who had signed the treaty gathered their followers and fled to Tampa Bay. There they asked the army to protect them.

Thompson could no longer ignore the signs of war.

More and more Seminoles were leaving their faraway villages to join Osceola. Women and children were disappearing from their villages, sent to hide in the shelter of the swamps.

Now Thompson gave these orders to the white traders: "No more rifles and bullets to the Indians."

His orders were not obeyed. There was a lot of money to be made selling guns to the Seminoles. And the Seminoles were willing to trade anything of value to get arms. They piled up more and more weapons.

There was another sign of the growing unrest. The news of what happened to Chief Charley Emanthla spread through Florida like wildfire.

Chief Emanthla favored removal to the West. One day he paid a visit to the whites to arrange protection for the departure of his tribe and to sell his cattle. The gold and silver he had been paid was wrapped safely in his handkerchief.

He started back to his village. But he never reached his chickee.

Osceola and twelve Seminoles lay hidden behind thick trees, waiting. When Chief Emanthla approached, they stepped out into the clearing.

Osceola accused Chief Emanthla of treason. Chief Emanthla had agreed to deliver Seminoles to the whites for them to be sent west and, to Osceola, this act of betrayal was punishable by death.

Osceola raised his rifle and fired.

Then he knelt down and removed from Chief

Emanthla's body the handkerchief filled with gold and silver coins. He threw the coins as far as he could, scattering them in every direction. Osceola forbid any of his people from touching them.

✖ ✖ ✖

To his enemies, Osceola was a fierce and cunning foe. To his people, he was a great

Osceola (c. 1800–1838).
Native American Seminole chief.

patriot. Many called him "the Spirit of War." To his wives and children, he was a kind and gentle husband and father. It was the custom of the Seminole Indians to take two wives. Osceola loved both his wives dearly.

According to legend, Osceola one day came to the trading post at Fort King with several companions and the younger of his wives. Her name in Seminole was Checho-ter. The white men called her Morning Dew. Her father was a Seminole chief. Her mother was believed to have been a black woman, so in the eyes of the white men, Morning Dew was a slave.

Allegedly, Osceola was inside the fort talking with Thompson when he heard a scream. He rushed outside and saw Morning Dew being carried away by slave catchers.

Thompson supposedly did nothing to save her.

Osceola was filled with rage. Helplessly, he watched the white men steal his wife.

Swiftly, Osceola mounted his horse and rode toward his village. Above the sound of the galloping hooves, Thompson is said to have heard Osceola's chilling cry: *"Yo-ho-ee-tchee!"*

It was the Seminole war cry.

5

THE WAR BEGINS

sceola's cry was not only a call to battle.

It was also a personal message to Thompson. For Osceola did not intend to let his wrongdoings go unavenged.

Osceola began to study every movement that Thompson made. Soon he knew that regularly the general went to dine with a friend, and that regularly he took the same path back to the fort.

On the morning of December 28, Thompson was walking as usual. But this time Osceola and a war party were waiting.

It was Osceola who struck down the general. And it was the Seminole war cry — *Yo-ho-ee-tchee!* — that Thompson heard as he fell dead.

Word now reached Osceola that American troops under the command of a Major Francis Dade were marching north from Tampa Bay to reinforce Fort King.

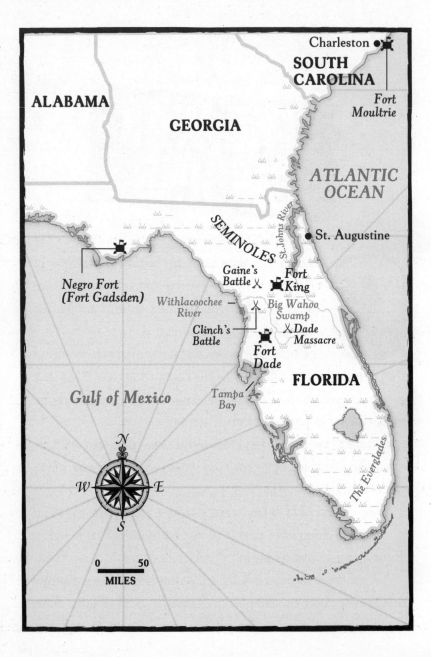

Charleston

**SOUTH
CAROLINA**

Fort
Moultrie

ALABAMA

GEORGIA

*ATLANTIC
OCEAN*

St. Johns River

SEMINOLES

• St. Augustine

Gaine's
Battle

Fort
King

**Negro Fort
(Fort Gadsden)**

*Withlacoochee
River*

*Big Wahoo
Swamp*

Clinch's
Battle

Dade
Massacre

Fort
Dade

FLORIDA

Gulf of Mexico

*Tampa
Bay*

N

W   E

S

The Everglades

0   50
MILES

This was what the Seminoles had long waited for — the chance to trap the enemy where they could not fight from the protection of a fort. Osceola and his warriors hurried south toward the Big Wahoo Swamp.

By the time Osceola arrived, the battle had been fought and won by the Seminoles. It had been a disaster for Dade and his men, and came to be known as the Dade Massacre.

Many times Osceola had told his warriors, "Show mercy. Act like men." Now the victorious Seminoles took all the ammunition they could lay their hands on. But they did not take a single scalp.

There was a victory celebration at the Big Wahoo Swamp that lasted three days. Then scouts came hurrying to the swamp with word that another army was approaching, this time led by General Duncan Clinch. There were many men, the scouts said — nearly eight hundred!

By the time General Clinch arrived with his army, not a Seminole was to be seen. The only sign of their presence was a canoe lying on its side in the water. General Clinch seized the canoe and put it to use ferrying his men to the other side of the Withlacoochee River.

About two hundred fifty of the soldiers had reached the other side of the river when suddenly the Seminoles came out from their hiding places and attacked. The general's army was now split in two. The five hundred men who were unable to cross the river watched helplessly as their comrades and the Seminoles fired at one another through the dense swamp grass.

Three times that day, General Clinch ordered his men into combat with fixed bayonets. Then, as they continued to fall before the Seminoles' fire, he called retreat.

The news flew: Dead! General Thompson. Dead! Major Dade and one hundred of his men. General Clinch, in retreat. All within three days!

6

A SEASON OF FEAR

apture every Seminole in Florida!" President Andrew Jackson ordered.

It was one thing to give orders from a government building in Washington. It was quite another thing to carry them out in the swamps of Florida.

Every Seminole was fighting this war to save their home and their people. Old men, women, girls, and boys too young to hold a rifle were all doing their part. They made bullets. They stored supplies. They cooked for the fighting male warriors.

Now another general was called in to direct the war, General Edmund Gaines. His plan was to take a stand on the banks of the Withlacoochee River. But when his men reached the river, they found themselves surrounded by Seminoles. The general's scouts reported that there were at least fourteen hundred. For days the soldiers were hemmed in, unable to cross the river.

During the night they could see the Seminole camp-fires and hear the battle cries of the warriors. General Gaines once caught a glimpse of Osceola, his face and body painted red, the Seminole color of war.

In desperation, Gaines sent a messenger to General Clinch. Somehow the man got through the tight Seminole lines and reached General Clinch. The message begged Clinch to send more troops immediately!

A week went by. Still Gaines waited for help. His men grew hungrier and hungrier. A little corn was all they had left. Soon the soldiers began to kill their horses for food.

One day, a man came to Gaines's camp with a message from Osceola. He wished to discuss peace. He wished to have a council. Eagerly, Gaines agreed.

Speaking at the council, Osceola said, "Our people are tired of fighting. We have lost many warriors. We wish for peace."

The general was also eager to have peace. He and the Seminole leaders began to discuss the terms on which the fighting could stop. Unfortunately, it was at this moment that General Clinch and the advance guard of his troops arrived.

General Clinch had marched his army north and south, looking for the elusive Seminoles. His men were hot and tired and angry. They came to the Withlacoochee

River and there at last were Seminoles. They fired.

Several Seminoles were killed. The rest of the Seminoles fled into the woods. They were sure they had been tricked again. Tricked at a peace council.

By nightfall, not one Seminole could be seen. Without a sign, without a sound, they had disappeared — more than a thousand of them — into the deepest shadows of the swamps.

Another general was called in to take command — General Winfield Scott. General Scott collected the largest army yet to gather in Florida.

He divided his men into three columns. His soldiers kept one another informed of their whereabouts by firing their cannons as signals.

Osceola and his warriors had to laugh at this. Did the white soldiers think that the Seminoles were born without ears? The bursts of cannon fire told them exactly where their enemy was at all times.

General Scott's men also searched in vain for the Seminoles' hiding places. These soldiers, too, were not used to this way of fighting a war. They were used to shelters, to open roads, to fighting the enemy face-to-face.

But this miserable country was without roads, without forts. Here the enemy remained hidden in secret marshland places.

The white soldiers found this maddening and frightening. What kind of fighting was this? They couldn't even *see* the enemy. They traded shots with shadows in a thicket of cypress. The Seminoles seemed to attack from nowhere. In small bands, they emerged from their hidden places in swamps and grasses, attacking swiftly, striking suddenly at the rear of the marching troops, and then disappearing once again.

In the same terrifying way, the Seminoles attacked army posts and settlements.

An attack by Seminoles on a U.S. blockhouse. The blockhouse was a small two-story structure made of heavy timbers. The sides are pierced with holes from which men fired on attackers. The top story was often used as an observation post.

All that winter the frontier was aflame. The people of Florida slept restlessly. Who could tell when a cabin or a barn would suddenly be set on fire?

Would they wake to see a band of armed Seminoles at their window?

It was a season of fear.

⊠ ⊠ ⊠

Then it was spring. And, for the Seminoles, it was a season of hunger. There had been no time to plant corn or to hunt game in the forest. Their cattle had long since been taken by the whites.

Sometimes the warriors told their women and children to stay hidden in the swamps. They dared not come out to hunt or fish. Sometimes the women and children went hungry for hours, even days, shivering in their wet, cold clothes.

They longed for their homes, their villages, their cornfields, and the gardens in their light, bright, sunlit world. Now their homes were the dark swamps where wild, tangled greens hid them from enemy eyes.

Sometimes, from the swamps where they lay hidden, they could hear the enemy coming close. Then quickly the Seminole women would bury their children in pits they had dug. They would cover the children's faces with palm leaves and warn them softly not to cry out. Only when all their children were safe would they look to themselves. Then they hid in the water, covering their faces with lily pads.

Yet great as their suffering was, the Seminoles would not give up.

General Scott was recalled to Washington, DC. President Jackson was furious that he had not ended the war. And a new general got his orders: General Richard Call.

General Call acted quickly. He sent for bloodhounds to help track down the Seminoles.

The newspaper in St. Augustine, Florida, reported: "We hope soon to hear they are on the scent of the enemy."

But it was not a war that could be won with dogs.

General Call's soldiers came to the jungle, the forest, and the swamp. They came sweating in the heat, cursing, and dragging their guns.

They did not know, as the Seminoles did, how to avoid the bogs where the deadly moccasin snake slithered, or the forests where the diamondback rattlesnake sounded its death warning. They learned — often too late — that the alligator was not the peaceful drifting log it seemed to be. At night, the air thickened with mosquitoes. Who could sleep with their constant biting and swarming?

General Call's men died as often from the bites of the snakes and the mosquitoes as they did from the weapons of the Seminoles.

Seminoles preparing to ambush U.S. troops.
First Seminole War, 1817.

In the wet summer months, disease came to the swamps. In June and July, malaria fever killed many Seminoles. The fever did not spare even "the Spirit of War." Osceola, too, was stricken.

Malaria killed hundreds of U.S. soldiers and weakened hundreds more. In Washington, DC, General Call's efforts to win the war had to be recorded as another failure.

7

THE PROMISE IS BROKEN

he Seminole War had to end. But how? Give Florida back to the Seminoles? Never! Then get the Seminoles out of Florida. Yes! But how? General after general had failed.

There was only one answer to this whole Seminole problem, said the government men. Osceola! Wasn't he the great "Spirit of War"? Kill the Spirit of War and end the war!

General Thomas Jesup was called in.

He was determined to do what other generals had failed to do. *He would win this war.* And he would capture Osceola.

Jesup was a cautious man. He went over his plans carefully. He would avoid sending large numbers of soldiers into the deadly swamps. He would make sure to have enough supplies.

He called upon the old enemy of the Seminoles, the

Creek Indians, to join him in battle. He promised the Creeks that they could take Black Seminoles as their prisoners — and then they could sell them as slaves.

He put his plans to work.

The soldiers and the Creeks entered the swamps and began their attack.

First, sixteen Black Seminoles were captured. Then thirty-six more. Then cattle and horses, ammunition and supplies. Then twenty-five more Seminoles — mostly women and children.

But what of Osceola? With each day that passed, General Jesup could think of little else. Where was Osceola?

Finally, Jesup sent a message to the Seminoles. The message offered peace if they would get out of Florida.

Once more, the chiefs agreed to meet. In his official report to the government, the general wrote: "I shall probably be able to follow the enemy into their most hidden retreats, should they reject the terms offered them."

The meeting took place, but Osceola was not there. The chiefs listened to the offer of peace. *They must leave Florida.* They had heard these words before.

Then suddenly, General Jesup was saying something new, something wonderfully different: *The Black Seminoles would be allowed to go west with the rest of the Seminole Nation.* Furthermore, Jesup said that the government would pay the Seminoles a fair price for their cattle and ponies. He promised to protect their lives and property.

The chiefs heard the offer with joy. After all these years, the rights of the Black Seminoles were going to be protected.

The chiefs agreed to this. They would gather all of their people together for the journey west.

When Osceola heard, he, too, agreed. But did the United States government really mean to carry out the promises that General Jesup had made? Most important was the promise that the Black Seminoles could also go in safety to the West.

The Seminoles began coming together at Tampa Bay. There, drifting at anchor, were the twenty-six boats waiting to move them on the first leg of their journey.

General Jesup was sure now that at last the war was over. But he had made his plans without discussing them with the slave catchers.

They, too, began gathering at Tampa Bay. When he learned of this, Jesup was angry. He wrote to the officer in command at Tampa Bay and ordered the slave owners to leave. The Seminoles did not wish to go to war again, he said, but any attempt to seize Black Seminoles "would be followed by an instant resort to arms."

But to the slave owners, the main purpose of this Second Seminole War was to capture Black Seminoles. When the slave owners heard that General Jesup had

American camp at Tampa Bay, Florida.

agreed to let the Black Seminoles go west, they raised a storm of protest. They went to Washington, DC, claiming that to end the war on such terms would be a clear triumph for the Seminoles.

General Jesup could not stand up against the slave owners and their powerful friends in the government. He gave in to their demands. He would try something else. "I have some hopes," he wrote, "of inducing both Indians and Indian negroes to unite in bringing in the negroes taken from the citizens during the war."

But who could tell which black people had run away, and which had always lived with the Seminole Nation?

The slave catchers could not tell, and it was clear they

did not care. They swarmed into the Tampa Bay area and seized anyone with black skin.

With Osceola in charge, all the Seminoles fled for their lives. One night, more than seven hundred chiefs, warriors, and their families disappeared into the safety of the swamps. And as they fled, they warned all others who were still planning to come to Tampa Bay to save themselves.

Newspapers all over the country blamed General Jesup for letting the Seminoles — especially Osceola — slip through his grasp.

The general had all of this war he could take. He asked permission to return to Washington, DC. His request was turned down. To the secretary of war he wrote, "To rid the country of them you must exterminate them. Is the government prepared for such a measure? Will public opinion sustain it?"

Then he wrote to a fellow officer in the army, "If you see Osceola again, tell him that I intend to send exploring parties into every part of the country this summer. I shall send out and take all the negroes who belong to the white people, and he must not allow the Indians or the Indian negroes to mix with them. Tell him I am sending . . . for bloodhounds to trail them and I intend to hang every one of them who does not come in."

Jesup also wrote to commanding officers at several army posts in Seminole territory. He told the military officers that they could take any captured Seminole's cattle or horses and consider them as their own property. Then came the heart of Jesup's message: The soldiers could sell any black person they captured.

So now the soldiers, too, became slave catchers. Two other Native American tribes even agreed to help the soldiers track the Seminoles down if they were paid $50 for each black person they caught. The Cherokee refused. "The Seminoles are our brothers," they said.

There followed another summer of sickness, hunger, and despair for the Seminoles.

Unlike the United States Army, the Seminoles could not replace a lost warrior. Their warriors were becoming fewer and fewer. Most of their cattle had already been taken. They could not plant crops in swamps. Osceola knew they were facing starvation. He himself was ill. How much longer could he lead his people?

8

THE WHITE FLAG DISHONORED

ne day, General Jesup received from Osceola the white plume of an egret and a peace pipe made of beads. Jesup knew what these two gifts meant. The pipe meant that Osceola wished to meet and talk of peace. The white feather meant that the Seminoles promised safety to the whites who came to the meeting ground.

The general knew this was his last chance to end the Seminole War and to emerge from this war a hero. He was prepared to use any method — fair or foul — to carry out his goal.

Once more he laid his plans.

He commanded his assistant, General Hernandez, to meet with Osceola twenty miles south of St. Augustine. He gave Hernandez a list of questions to be put to Osceola. If Osceola's replies were not satisfactory, Hernandez knew what he was to do.

The eventful day was October 21, 1837.

Osceola and the other Seminole leaders put on their full ceremonial dress and shining silver jewelry. In their turbans they placed plumes of the egret to show they were meeting in peace. The white flag of truce that was flying in the gentle Florida breeze told Osceola that the white man was also meeting in peace. Like the plume of the egret, the flag of truce was a bond that no honorable man would betray.

Osceola and Hernandez greeted each other with friendly gestures. The Seminoles were asked to disarm. Osceola told his people to stack their weapons, and they did.

This was to be a meeting to talk peace. But the first question General Hernandez asked was: "Are you prepared to deliver up the negroes taken from the citizens?"

Osceola was stunned. He turned to the chief at his side and in a shaking voice said, "I am choked; you must speak for me. . . ."

But there was no time for anyone to speak. Hernandez gave a signal. His troops, hidden nearby, moved in. Osceola was captured, together with twelve chiefs, seventy-five warriors, and six women.

One of the soldiers later wrote to a friend, "I shall never forget that day, nor the sad, disappointed face of Chief Osceola and the other Indians. We were outraged by the cowardly way he was betrayed into capture."

But General Jesup sat down and wrote to the secretary of war, "I have the satisfaction to inform you that Osceola is my prisoner."

It was not a satisfaction that was shared by the American people. Newspapers across the nation reported in outrage the shameful capture of Osceola:

"Dishonorable."

"A violation of all that is noble and generous in war."

"We cannot forget that he was provoked by treachery and captured by treachery."

Osceola being seized at Fort Peyton, Florida, October 21, 1837.

9

NO WORD FOR GOOD-BYE

 n the damp prison, Osceola was slowly dying. Yet so important a prisoner was he that when one of the Seminole chiefs escaped, Osceola was taken to a safer fortress. In December 1837, he was sent to Fort Moultrie near Charleston, South Carolina.

The story of Osceola spread across the land. More and more Americans were learning of his fight for his people, and many became sympathetic toward his struggle.

Sometimes a guard would take Osceola out of his prison cell and let him sit by the water's edge. Sad and silent, Osceola watched the gulls swoop low, saw the blue herons fly over the grasses. He sat there motionless and heard the wind whisper through the trees. The gull, the heron, the wind — all free, but not Osceola.

Many people came to South Carolina to see the famous prisoner. Among them was George Catlin of

Osceola. A painting by George Catlin.

Pennsylvania. He was one of the most famous painters in America, and he had come to paint Osceola's portrait. Osceola dressed in his finest clothes for the portrait.

During his time in prison, Osceola also spoke with a journalist named Thomas Storrow. Osceola told him, "It was always my pride to fight with the '*big generals*.'" Then, pointing to his clothes, Osceola said, "I wore this plume when I whipped General Gaines, these spurs when I drove back General Clinch, and these moccasins when I flogged General Call."

On January 30, Osceola knew that he was dying. He could no longer speak, but with his hands he called for his chiefs and the military officers of the fort. He would die as he had lived — in dignity.

With difficulty, he pulled on his buckskin tunic, his leggings, and his moccasins. He put on his war belt and carefully laid the war knife in its sheath by his side.

Then he called for red paint. Slowly, and without using a mirror, he painted one half of his face and throat. Then he painted his wrists and the backs of his hand with the red paint of war. He smoothed the feathers in his turban and placed it upon his thick black hair.

Exhausted, he lay back upon his bed to rest for a moment. Then, with great effort, he smiled and held out his hand. The Seminoles and the whites came up to take his hand in silent farewell.

He lay still. Those standing near him thought him dead. But slowly his hand moved to his war belt and he drew out his knife. A deep silence filled the room as he laid the knife against his breast.

A moment later, he died.

There is no word for "good-bye" in the Seminole language.

At the age of thirty-four, Osceola was dead. But the war went on. For four more terrible years, the Seminoles led the fever-ridden troops on an exhausting chase from swamp to swamp.

Finally, most of the Seminoles, hungry and homeless, agreed to be moved west — Seminole and Black Seminole together.

But some three hundred Seminoles refused to come out of the swamps. Those Seminoles were not strong enough to continue to fight, but they never signed a peace treaty with the United States.

Osceola is buried at Fort Moultrie in South Carolina. Above his grave, there is a marker that was placed there by the nation that fought him.

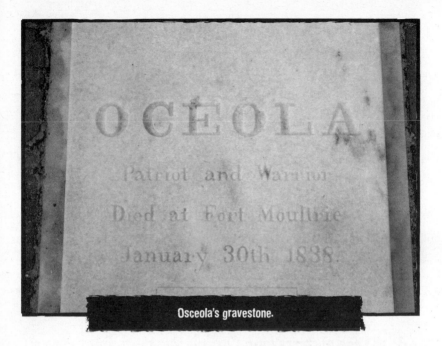

Osceola's gravestone.

Today, deep in the Florida Everglades, wild animals still roam the woods. Many fish and alligators still swim in the rivers. Snakes slither over the ground and birds fly overhead.

And there are still Seminoles there — the great-great-grandchildren of the proud Seminole warriors who refused to surrender, who were never defeated.

More than one hundred years later, in 1970, the Seminole Indians were awarded money by the U.S. government for the Florida land they had been forced to give up. They were awarded approximately twelve million dollars. It was said that the land that was taken from them was worth almost fifty million dollars.

INDIANS ARE AWARDED CASH IN LAW SUIT

WASHINGTON(AP) — The Seminole Indians, who owned most of Florida 150 years ago, were awarded $12,347,500 Wednesday for land taken from them by U.S. military forces.

The award—from which will be deducted past payments of money and land—was made by the Indian Claims Commission on the basis of what it determined the land was worth a century and a half ago.

The decision, unless appealed to the U.S. Court of Claims, ends one of the longest and bitterest Indian disputes in the nation's history. The suit was filed 20 years ago.

The award was considerably less than the Indians had hoped for. The Seminoles contended in hearings last June that the 29.7 million acres taken from them—covering most of Florida's now high-cost land—was worth $47.9 million. Government appraisers set the value at $5.5 million.

The government estimates offset costs at more than $5 million. Offsets are what the government claims has been spent on the Indians or given them as a result of treaties and should be deducted from the commission's award.

The Seminoles' troubles began in 1816 when Gen. Andrew Jackson invaded Florida with federal troops to punish them for hiding fugitive slaves. Troubles continued after the United States bought Florida from Spain. The Indians claimed Spain never owned it, so the United States couldn't legally buy it.

The Indians went on the warpath to protect their rights and later, they contended, were tricked into two separate treaties in 1823 and 1832.

While many resettled in Oklahoma, others escaped into the cypress swamps of the Florida Everglades where they have lived ever since.

The second Seminole War broke out in 1835 after many Seminoles refused to move to Oklahoma. Chief Osceola, tricked into surrendering, died in a federal prison in 1838.

Two decades ago, after Congress had established the Indian Claims Commission, the Seminoles asked for compensation for the lands taken.

The chief value of the land 150 years ago was for agriculture and for the native oak and the rare red mahogany trees which were much in demand for building ships.

In 1964, the commission ruled that the Seminoles did own title to most of Florida in 1823 and were entitled to compensation.

The Post and Courier, Thursday, May 14, 1970.

TECUMSEH

Tecumseh. A portrait based on descriptions of the Shawnee chief.

1

THE YOUNG TECUMSEH

n Old Piqua, a village of wigwams and bark cabins near the Mad River of Ohio, Tecumseh was born. From the time of his birth in March 1768, to the time of his death forty-five years later, there would be little peace for Tecumseh and his people, the Shawnee Nation.

While Tecumseh was still a very young child his father taught him many skills. Before he was six he had learned how to make a bow for his arrows, how to throw the tomahawk, how to fish and hunt.

Tecumseh's father was not always home to teach him. For his father was a Shawnee warrior and was often away fighting the white settlers who came into the Shawnee land south of the Ohio River.

By the time Tecumseh was six years old, war had broken out between these settlers and the Shawnees. The fighting was fierce and both sides lost many men.

In the end the Shawnee commander, Chief Cornstalk, was forced to sign a treaty of peace. In this treaty, the Shawnees had to give up all their land south of the Ohio River.

Settlers from Virginia swarmed into this land that had been taken from the Shawnees. So the Shawnees retreated to the land north of the Ohio River. This would now be their home. The treaty promised that no settlers would come into this northern land.

It was a promise quickly broken. The settlers pressed on, wanting still more land to build farms and towns. In spite of the treaty, they seized Shawnee land north of the Ohio River.

XXX

When Tecumseh was six years old, his father died during a battle, fighting against the English colonists.

Tecumseh would always remember his mother's voice telling him to avenge the death of his father. A few months later, Tecumseh's seventh sibling — a boy, Laulewasika — was born. Soon after, Tecumseh's mother went west with many other members of her tribe, leaving the care of her baby and her other children to Tecumseh's older sister.

It was not long before Tecumseh lost another important person in his life.

Above all other men, Tecumseh had always admired

Chief Cornstalk, war leader of the Shawnees. Cornstalk had been at peace with the British colonists since the signing of the treaty. Then Tecumseh heard that Cornstalk had been killed while visiting an American fort. A mob of soldiers, angered by the killing of a white man, had shot the Shawnee leader.

Shawnee leader Cornstalk (c. 1720–November 10, 1777). A prominent leader of the Shawnee people.

XXX

Near Old Piqua was the village of Old Chillicothe, ruled by Chief Blackfish. It was fortunate for Tecumseh that Blackfish now adopted the lonely boy and treated him as his own son. Tecumseh divided his time between the two villages.

According to legend, it was his sister who taught him to be honest, to respect the rights of others, and to obey his elders.

Both Blackfish and Tecumseh's older brother taught him valuable skills of warfare.

In Old Piqua and Old Chillicothe, it is said that the elderly people took Tecumseh into their cabins and wigwams and taught him how to speak his thoughts clearly and with force.

The older Shawnees were grateful for Tecumseh's kindness to them. When the cold, harsh winds of winter began to blow, the young boy went from one village to the other, patching the old people's wigwams and cabins, bringing them meat to eat and deerskins to make warm clothing and moccasins.

But this small time of peace did not last.

Tecumseh was just a boy of eight when, in 1776, the Americans began their War of Independence against the British. The British promised not to take Native American land, so many Indian Nations fought alongside the British. The Shawnees, too, fought the Americans.

In 1780, the war came to Old Piqua. Tecumseh watched his village vanish in flames, as American soldiers drove the Shawnees from their homes.

In 1782, Tecumseh took part in his first battle.

Here, according to legend, Tecumseh saw his older brother wounded. Frightened, he fled from the battlefield. That night he called himself a coward and vowed he would never again show fear. From that day on, Tecumseh would be the last to leave the field of battle.

The Revolutionary War ended in 1783. With the end of the war came a new stream of settlers moving west. They came in greater and greater numbers, taking more and more Native American land in the north. The Shawnees fought to hold on to their hunting lands, to keep the settlers out. Tecumseh, twenty at the time, joined the band of Shawnees who attacked the flatboats carrying the settlers down the Ohio River.

After one such attack on a group of settlers' boat, the Shawnees burned a captive at the stake. Tecumseh watched with horror. He hated the white men with all his being. What had white men brought to his people but suffering? But he also knew compassion, and senseless torture sickened him.

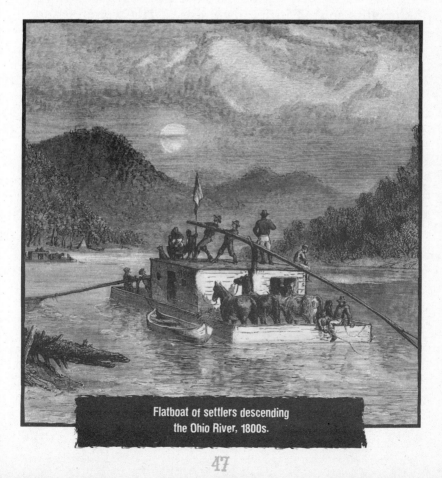

Flatboat of settlers descending the Ohio River, 1800s.

Legend has it that, suddenly, without a thought to his age or to his lesser place in the tribe, he was on his feet, crying to the older men that what they had done was not an act of courage nor an act of men. "An animal shows such cruelty to the helpless," he cried. "A man does not!"

The older men were shamed by the words of this twenty-year-old warrior.

Tecumseh began to learn the power of his own thoughts spoken in his own words. His words would come to be a powerful weapon to sway men and change the course of history.

2
A LEADER GROWS

nto the Northwest Territory, into Shawnee land, came the settlers. By boat and by wagon, in carts and on foot they came — ten thousand a year. And as the number of settlers grew, so grew Tecumseh's leadership in the Shawnee struggle to hold on to their land.

By the time Tecumseh was twenty-three, he had taken part in many battles against the frontiersmen.

The settlers turned to General Arthur St. Clair for help against the native people. In 1791, General St. Clair led an army of about a thousand men to the Wabash River. The Shawnees destroyed St. Clair's army in the battle that followed, and Tecumseh aided those who first broke through the American lines. This was so great a defeat for the Americans that for a long while, settlers were discouraged from coming to the Northwest Territory.

The following year, Tecumseh's older brother, Chief Cheeseekau, traveled south to help the Cherokee Indians fight the settlers in Tennessee. Cheeseekau sent word for Tecumseh to join him, and he did. When Chief Cheeseekau was killed in 1792, Tecumseh replaced him as leader of all the Shawnee warriors in the South. Tecumseh led them in battle in Tennessee, Mississippi, Alabama, Georgia, and Florida.

Two years later, still another brother was killed at Fallen Timbers. There, the mighty army of General "Mad" Anthony Wayne defeated the hopelessly outnumbered native people. Not satisfied with victory, General Wayne burned Native American villages, one after the other. After the Battle of Fallen Timbers, Wayne called for a council at Greenville, Ohio.

General Wayne's victory at the Battle of Fallen Timbers, opening the Ohio Valley for settlers, 1794.

To this council came a thousand Native Americans from twelve different tribes. They signed a treaty in which they had to give up two-thirds of Ohio. In exchange for their land, the native people received $20,000 in goods and the promise of an additional $10,000.

Tecumseh had refused to go to the council at Greenville. He refused to take part in the giving up of this Native American land. He would not accept what the other chiefs had done. They had no right to sell the land of their fathers.

Tecumseh spoke against the treaty at every opportunity. Though he was only twenty-seven, he spoke with the wisdom and power of a great chief, and more and more Native Americans listened.

A year later, while visiting his sister in Ohio, Tecumseh came to know the settler James Galloway and his family. It is said that Galloway had brought three hundred books to his wilderness home and that Tecumseh was curious about them and interested to know what they contained.

It was Galloway's daughter, Rebecca, who became his teacher. In time, Tecumseh learned to speak and read English with ease. Eagerly, he read Galloway's books. For Tecumseh was thirsty for any knowledge that would help him better understand and deal with the white man.

After a time, Rebecca came to think of Tecumseh as the most remarkable man she had ever met. And

Tecumseh began to think of her as a woman he wanted to marry.

Following the Shawnee custom, Tecumseh supposedly asked James Galloway for permission to marry his daughter. Galloway liked Tecumseh. He thought him the most intelligent man he had ever met. He advised Tecumseh to ask Rebecca himself.

It is said that Rebecca agreed to marry Tecumseh — but only on one condition. He must give up his life as a Shawnee Indian. He must be willing to live as a white man.

Tecumseh needed time to think. He searched his mind and his heart. Then he made his decision.

He returned to Rebecca and told her he could not leave his people. He was a Shawnee Indian. He did not want to live as a white man.

3

"MAKE THE SUN STAND STILL"

ecumseh's people were pushed farther and farther west as more settlers came from the East. Farmers, workers, old soldiers, outlaws, and adventurers came, paying two dollars an acre for farmland where the Native Americans had lived. They laid out towns where the native people had hunted.

With the white men came their whiskey. Tecumseh saw what whiskey did to his people. He saw how it destroyed their bodies and how it turned brother against brother.

Tecumseh heard terrible stories about his youngest brother, Laulewasika, whom he had not seen since childhood. He learned that Laulewasika had struggled with drinking for many years.

Then, in 1805, Tecumseh heard something even stranger about his brother. He heard that Laulewasika had given up whiskey and turned to religion. Laulewasika now called himself Tenskwatawa ("The Open Door") and claimed a hundred followers. The white settlers called him the Shawnee Prophet.

Tecumseh had to see this for himself. He went to his brother's village. There he heard Laulewasika tell his people to stop warring among themselves and to stop drinking the white man's whiskey.

Tecumseh saw the faces of his brother's followers. He saw that they believed every word his brother said.

Members of the United Society of Believers. They are called Shakers because when they worship, they tremble and chant a wordless song. The Shawnee Prophet may have been influenced by Shaker missionaries.

For some time now, Tecumseh had a dream — a hope that if all the Indian Nations from many tribes could come together to form *one* confederation, they would be better able to protect their land against the oncoming white settlers.

Tecumseh saw how Laulewasika could help with his plan. He and his brother joined forces. They would unite all the Nations in the land. Then they could keep the white men from taking any more of their country!

The two brothers moved to Greenville, Ohio, where the chiefs had signed the hated Treaty of Greenville in 1795.

XXX

In 1800, the westernmost part of the Northwest Territory became known as the Indiana Territory. William Henry Harrison, who would later become president of the United States, was made governor of this newly formed territory. Governor Harrison became worried as more and more of the Shawnee Prophet's followers came to Greenville. Too many native people in one place might mean trouble. Perhaps if he could weaken the Shawnee Prophet's power, he could disperse the Native Americans.

He had a plan. In April 1806, Governor Harrison sent a message to the Delaware Indians (also known as the Lenape Indians): "If he is really a prophet," he said, "ask him to cause the sun to stand still, the moon to alter its course, the rivers to cease to flow or the dead to rise from their graves. If he does these things, you may then believe he has been sent from God."

Harrison's challenge excited the Shawnee Prophet. He would use the challenge to help unite the Nations.

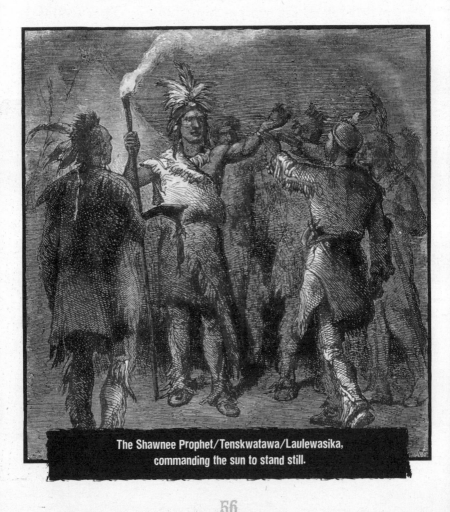

The Shawnee Prophet/Tenskwatawa/Laulewasika, commanding the sun to stand still.

The Shawnee Prophet found out that there was soon to be a total eclipse of the sun. He even knew the day on which the scientists expected the eclipse — June 16.

He sent word to the Nations that the Shawnee Prophet would cause the sun to darken, and that they could all witness this miracle themselves.

On June 16, a great crowd came to Greenville, Ohio. The Shawnee Prophet appeared, dressed in dark, flowing robes.

He pointed to the sun. At noontime, the moon began to move slowly across the face of the sun. In the growing darkness, the people looked at one another wordlessly and gazed at the Shawnee Prophet in awe. Then the Shawnee Prophet cried out to his "Master of Life." He asked that He uncover the sun to let it shine once more.

When light returned and the sun shone brightly, the crowds stole silently away, too full of wonder to speak.

News of the Shawnee Prophet's power spread like a wind across the land. Soon more and more Native Americans joined him in Greenville.

Tecumseh's chance had come at last. Together with his brother, the Shawnee Prophet, he would unite all tribes into a single force with a singular purpose — to defend *their* land.

THE WARRIOR AND THE GOVERNOR

ow was the time, Tecumseh believed, to go among the native people of the East, West, South, and North, and to urge them to unite.

But first, Tecumseh thought, the Shawnee Prophet's village at Greenville would have to be moved elsewhere. Greenville was too close to white settlements and every move made by the Native Americans was watched and reported to Governor Harrison.

So a new village, called Prophetstown, was built. It was set up where the Wabash and the Tippecanoe Rivers joined, closer to Harrison but farther from his informers.

In the spring of 1808, Tecumseh and his brother traveled across the central plains, stopping now with one group, moving on to another. At every council fire, Tecumseh spoke and his words stirred those who listened:

"The annihilation of our race is at hand unless we unite in one common cause against the common foe. . . . Every year our white intruders become more greedy, exacting, oppressive and overbearing."

"Let us form one body, one heart, and defend to the last warrior our country, our homes, our liberty, and the graves of our fathers."

To the Nations along the Illinois River, to the Nations of Wisconsin, Tecumseh spoke again and again of his plan for an Indian Federation so strong and so united that it could defend its land.

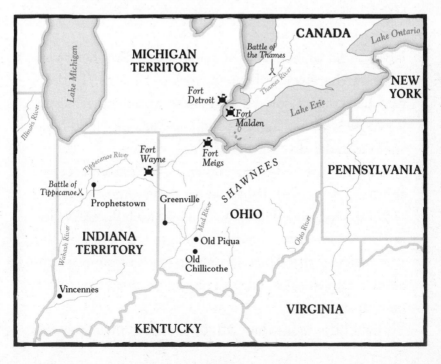

In many villages those who listened welcomed this idea. Some chiefs, however, wanted nothing to do with war. Others feared they would lose the leadership of their tribe.

Tecumseh traveled thousands of miles — to Florida to speak to the Seminoles, to Missouri where the Osage tribes gathered to listen to him, and finally to New York and the Iroquois.

He felt he had made progress in the year of his travels. Though his ideas were not accepted everywhere, he had sowed the seeds for the greatest Indian Federation in the history of his people.

⊠ ⊠ ⊠

Now, as he turned toward Indiana and Prophetstown, he knew there was still much work to be done. To those who had turned down his ideas, he would appeal again. To those who had agreed to follow him, he would come again to make sure they would not weaken.

On the way back to Indiana, Tecumseh received shocking news. While he had been away, in the summer of 1809, Governor Harrison had met with several chiefs at Fort Wayne and convinced them to sign a new treaty. It is believed that Harrison may have first supplied the chiefs with whiskey and then pressured them to sign this new treaty.

For a little more than $10,000, these chiefs had sold

three million acres of Native American land. Much of it owned by Nations whose chiefs were not even at Fort Wayne! With the lost land went some of the Shawnees' best hunting grounds.

Tecumseh felt that the land these chiefs sold had rightfully belonged to all the Indians, and that no one chief had the right to sell any of it. Tecumseh sent word to Nations near and far that he refused to honor the treaty of Fort Wayne. By the spring of 1810, a thousand warriors had flocked to Prophetstown, ready to fight if the white men tried to settle on the land.

Tecumseh decided on a bold action. He would go to Vincennes, Indiana, to confront the governor.

On August 11, 1810, Tecumseh, the Shawnee Prophet, and dozens of armed warriors arrived in canoes at Vincennes. The warriors had painted their faces red, the color of war.

The meeting was to take place at a grove near the governor's headquarters. Tecumseh picked seventy-five of his warriors to accompany him and his brother to the meeting. Many important officials were already there.

Tecumseh was the first to speak. He directed his words to Governor Harrison. He went over the history of every treaty ever made with the Native Americans and told how unfair each treaty proved to be. He spoke of what took place after the treaties were signed — how the native people who were supposed to be protected by the treaties were killed, how their land was taken away, how they were given spoiled food, how death had come to many after they were exposed to smallpox, a disease unknown to the native people before the white man came.

He spoke of his plan to unite the Native Americans:

> **"Your states have set an example of forming a union. . . . Why should you censure the Indians for following that example?"**

> **"Sell a country? Why not sell the air, the clouds, and the Great Sea as well as the earth? Did not the Great Spirit make them all for the use of his children?"**

> **"The only way to stop this evil is for all the red men to unite in claiming an equal right in the land. . . . No groups among us have a right to sell, even to one another, and surely not to outsiders who want all and will not do with less."**

Then Harrison began to speak. He claimed that the United States had always been fair in dealing with the Native Americans.

At these words, Tecumseh leaped to his feet. He was horrified by this false claim, and supposedly called Harrison a liar. The moment was tense. The governor drew his sword from its sheath and stepped forward. Tecumseh's warriors drew their tomahawks from their belts and awaited their leader's signal.

Shawnee chief Tecumseh confronting Governor William Henry Harrison in Indiana.

Harrison declared that the council was over. Without another word, he walked toward his headquarters.

Tecumseh led his warriors back to their camp. The next morning he sent apologies for his outburst to Governor Harrison.

The governor accepted the apology and came to visit Tecumseh at his camp. Tecumseh invited him to sit on a bench beside him. As they talked, Tecumseh moved closer to Harrison. The governor was forced to move farther down the bench. Again, Tecumseh moved closer. Again, Harrison moved away. This went on until the governor was at the end of the bench. Tecumseh was trying to show Harrison how the Native Americans felt to be pushed off of their own land.

5

"LET US UNITE"

he end of the Revolutionary War had not brought lasting peace to Great Britain and America. It looked as if they would soon be at war with each other again.

Tecumseh felt the British could help his people fight the American soldiers. He went to Fort Malden, the British outpost in Canada. There he talked to a British Native American agent named Colonel Matthew Elliott about his Indian Federation. He asked for arms and supplies in case America and Great Britain went to war. He felt that the meeting was a success. Back home, he told his people the British had promised to help them.

It was time, Tecumseh felt, to journey to the South once more to meet with the Native American nation. And on August 5, 1811, he set off down the Wabash River with twenty warriors by his side.

His journey took him down the Ohio and Mississippi Rivers, through Tennessee to Mississippi, Alabama,

Georgia, Florida, back up north to the Carolinas, to the Ozark Mountains of Arkansas and Missouri, and north into Iowa. He traveled by pony, in canoe, and on foot.

Sometimes as many as five thousand Indians gathered to listen to him. He spoke to the Choctaws and the Chickasaws, urging them to live in peace with all the other Indians. He told how the Americans were grabbing up land. He asked that the tribes fight on the side of the British should there be another war between the United States and Great Britain.

His words were forceful:

> "Where today are the . . . once powerful tribes of our people? . . . Look over their once beautiful country and what see you now? Nothing but the ruins of the paleface destroyers! So it will be with you, Chocktaws and Chickasaw! Soon your mighty forests . . . will be cut down to fence in the land which the white intruders dare to call their own!"

And to the Creek Indians, he cried:

> "[You] were once a mighty people. . . . Now your tomahawks have no edge, your bows and arrows were buried with your fathers. Brush from your eyelids the sleep of slavery! Once more strike for vengeance — once more for your country!"

His speech was moving. Half the warriors were ready

to join him. But the chief of the Upper Creeks did not agree with Tecumseh. He would not approve Tecumseh's Indian Federation.

"This is the will of the Great Spirit, revealed to my brother . . . He sends me to you," Tecumseh cried in anger. "I will stamp my foot at Tippecanoe, and the very earth shall shake."

On the night of December 16, 1811, a rumbling was heard and the Mississippi Valley shook from an earthquake. The Creeks whispered in awe, and the word was passed from one tribe to another that Tecumseh had reached the Tippecanoe River.

Tecumseh remained on the move. He traveled south to the village of the Seminoles who swore to join him. But he had no such luck with the Cherokee or the Osage or the Iowa Indians.

He headed for home, footsore and heartsick, still unable to unite all his people. He had traveled thousands of miles in six months. Mountains and swamps had not stopped him. Rain and snow had not slowed him.

Wearily he reached Prophetstown on a cold gray day in 1812.

He could not believe his eyes. Prophetstown was in ruins — the fields burned, the wigwams and council house destroyed.

That night, Tecumseh found out what had happened. General Harrison had waited until Tecumseh left on his journey. Then he marched his army to Prophetstown.

The Shawnees feared Harrison's attack and knew they were hopelessly outnumbered. Tecumseh had very clearly instructed his brother, the Shawnee Prophet, to avoid any conflict with Harrison since he did not think they could win against his soldiers, or at least not until he returned. There was disagreement among the warriors, however. Some felt their only hope was to launch a surprise attack of their own. And they did.

The Shawnees had approximately five hundred men; the Americans more than a thousand. The battle — called the Battle of Tippecanoe — which lasted only a day, was a victory for Harrison and his army. But before

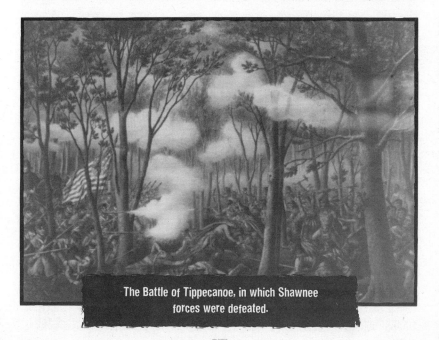

The Battle of Tippecanoe, in which Shawnee forces were defeated.

he returned to Vincennes, General Harrison destroyed Prophetstown.

Not satisfied with smashing the houses, Harrison's army also destroyed all of the corn the Shawnees had harvested. Tippecanoe was not a big battle, but Harrison turned it into a great victory for himself. He wrote to the secretary of war: "The Indians had never sustained so severe a defeat since their acquaintance with the white people." Later, when Harrison ran for president of the United States, John Tyler was his candidate for vice president. Their campaign slogan was "Tippecanoe and Tyler too." It helped them get elected.

"Tippecanoe and Tyler too," the campaign slogan used by William Henry Harrison when he ran for the office of president. Harrison's campaign was known for torchlight parades, hard cider, and barbecues.

The defeat at Tippecanoe was a terrible blow to Tecumseh. He had lost his headquarters, his supplies, almost everything. It was the kind of small warfare he had hoped to avoid. He wanted to fight the soldiers when he could have a strong, united Indian Federation.

He gathered his people around him where the council house once stood. And he made this vow:

> **"I stand upon the ashes of my home. I summon the spirits of the braves who have fallen as they protected their homes. I swear once more the hatred of an avenger."**

Tecumseh held his brother, the Shawnee Prophet, responsible for the tragedy.

Tecumseh had told him again and again that there was to be no fighting until he returned. The Shawnee Prophet had not followed orders to prevent the battle.

The Shawnee Prophet soon wandered west, his followers and his influence gone.

6

IN THE ARMY OF THE KING

he War of 1812 between America and Great Britain was declared on June 18, 1812. Most Native Americans, including Tecumseh, sided with the British. Tecumseh explained his reasons:

"Here is a chance . . . that will never occur again, a chance for us Indians of North America to form ourselves into one great combination and cast our lot with the British in this war. Should they conquer and again get mastery of the whole of North America, our rights to at least a portion of the land of our fathers would be respected by the King. If they should not win and the whole country should pass into the hands of the [Americans] . . . it will not be many years before our last hunting ground will be taken from us."

Thousands of warriors from many tribes came to join Tecumseh in the battles that followed.

Major-General Isaac Brock took command of Fort Malden in Canada on August 13. His first action was to call a meeting of his top officers. When Brock and Tecumseh were introduced, they shook hands in friendship. Tecumseh felt that he could place his confidence in the tall, rugged general, and Brock saw immediately the qualities that made Tecumseh a great leader.

Brock asked the officers what they thought the British should do next. "Attack Fort Detroit," Tecumseh said. He knew that the American general William Hull had more than two thousand soldiers at Fort Detroit. He also knew that General Hull was not a fighter and that he would be terrified by a sudden attack. With the point of his knife, Tecumseh drew a map of Fort Detroit on a piece of elm bark and described its defenses.

Brock listened to the arguments of the other men. Only one of the officers agreed with Tecumseh that Fort Detroit could be captured.

Brock made up his mind quickly. He would follow Tecumseh's plan. The British and the Native Americans together would plan an attack on Fort Detroit.

Under a great oak tree on a broad meadow just outside Fort Malden, General Brock faced Tecumseh's warriors.

"Welcome to the army of the Great King," he began. Then he told them that the Americans wanted to drive not only the native people but the British from the land as well. He told them he meant to carry the war across the river. He would help recover their land.

Then Tecumseh spoke. "The Americans are our enemies," he said. He continued to speak:

> "They came to us hungry and they cut off the hands of our brothers who gave them corn. We gave them rivers of fish, and they poisoned our fountains. We gave them forest-clad mountains and valleys full of game, and in return what did they give our warriors and our women? Rum and trinkets and a grave!"

On the afternoon of August 14, Brock and Tecumseh led their armies north.

Tecumseh and his warriors crossed the river. They surrounded Fort Detroit, cutting off all approaches by land.

Brock took Tecumseh aside and told him of a trick he had played. He had let a British messenger be captured by the Americans on purpose. The British messenger told General Hull that a war party of five thousand Indians was coming to fight against him.

Tecumseh smiled. He would add further trickery to Brock's plan. He assembled his entire force of six hundred Native Americans and told them what to do. Immediately the woods were filled with terrifying war whoops. Three times, the Native Americans ran back and forth, four and five abreast, in full view of the American fort. The running Native Americans, seen first in one place, then in another, convinced General Hull that there were at least five thousand men ready to charge from the forest.

Hull ordered the white flag of surrender raised over Fort Detroit.

Brock and Tecumseh were stunned. They had expected a fierce fight and had not been at all sure of defeating an army twice the size of their own. It was a great victory for Brock and Tecumseh.

The British major-general understood the part the Shawnee chief had played in the victory. As their soldiers and warriors watched, Brock gave Tecumseh his own silk sash and his pair of beautiful pistols. Tecumseh presented Brock with a beaded belt, which the general kept for the rest of his life.

Map of the city of Detroit showing the location of Fort Detroit.

7

"I AM TECUMSEH"

eneral Brock moved his headquarters to a house in Detroit, and Tecumseh was given a parlor and a bedroom on the second floor.

The days that followed were among the few peaceful times Tecumseh knew in his life. He laughed a lot, smoked his pipe, and enjoyed pleasant meals with the officers.

In his report, Brock wrote of Tecumseh: "A more gallant warrior does not exist. He has the admiration of everyone who talks with him."

But the peaceful days were soon to end. Brock left for the Niagara border to stop an American invasion there. He left Colonel Henry Procter in charge of Detroit.

Procter and Brock were as different as night and day. Many believed Procter was a vain, slow-thinking man who thought a great deal of himself and very little of the native people.

Tecumseh knew he would have trouble with Procter. And soon after Brock had left Detroit, trouble arose.

Procter ordered that the citizens of Detroit would have to swear loyalty to the British Crown. One of the leading Americans in Detroit was Father Gabriel, a priest and a friend to the native people. He refused. "I have taken one oath to support the Constitution of the United States," he said, "and I cannot take another. Do with me as you please."

Procter threw him into prison.

Tecumseh demanded that Procter release the prisoner. If Procter did not, Tecumseh would take all of his warriors back to the Wabash River. "General Brock would understand my reasons," Tecumseh said.

Procter quickly ordered Father Gabriel set free.

But even though Tecumseh had won this small victory, he knew that he had only increased the bad feelings between himself and the colonel.

In September 1812, Tecumseh began another journey south. He thought that if the Creek Indians could wage war in the South, the Americans would have two wars on their hands and chance of success would be greater.

Once more the Creeks listened to Tecumseh's words. He reminded them of how they had been successful in the North. And he told them that the British were now their allies. Tecumseh spoke of how it was the British who would let them keep their land; and of how it was the Americans who sought to take it away. The Creeks were now ready to follow Tecumseh and fight beside the British.

When Tecumseh returned to Fort Malden, Ontario, in April of 1813, he led three thousand warriors. Never before had the Native Americans brought together such an army. All they needed was an able British commander.

The news Tecumseh received on his return made his heart heavy with sorrow. His good friend, Major-General Brock, had been killed in battle. And the man he despised, Colonel Procter, was now in command, promoted to general.

The British and the Native Americans were soon to face Tecumseh's old enemy, General Harrison. How could a man like Procter lead them to victory?

The battle took place at Fort Meigs. Once more, Tecumseh resorted to trickery. Though his warriors numbered thirteen hundred, he sent this message to General Harrison:

> **"I have with me eight hundred braves. You have an equal number in your hiding place. Come out with them and give me battle. You talked like a brave when we met at Vincennes . . . but now you hide behind logs, and in the earth, like a groundhog. Give me your answer."**

No answer came from the fort. Nevertheless, Tecumseh led an attack on the Americans and he was successful. But when he returned to the fort, he came upon a scene that filled him with rage. A group of Native Americans was torturing twenty American soldiers.

Tecumseh charged at them at a gallop. He grabbed a knife from one warrior and sent others sprawling to the ground. Standing between the native people and their prisoners, he shouted, "Are there no men here?"

Tecumseh was heartsick. He blamed Procter for doing nothing to stop the torture.

Tecumseh stormed into the general's tent, demanding to know why the general had not prevented the torturing of the Americans.

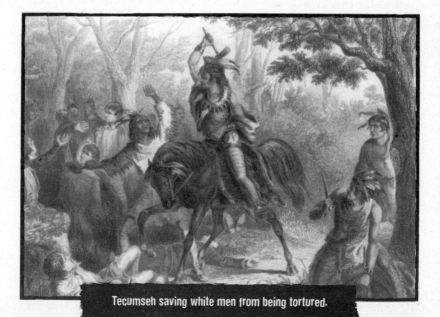

Tecumseh saving white men from being tortured.

"Your Indians cannot be controlled," Procter said, in his haughtiest tone. "They cannot be commanded."

"You are not fit to command!" Tecumseh cried. "Go put on petticoats."

Later, Procter tried to get back at Tecumseh for insulting him by issuing orders that the native people be given horsemeat to eat instead of beef.

When Tecumseh heard about this, he went to see Procter. He didn't bother to explain to Procter that it was Tecumseh and his warriors who were carrying the heavy load of this war. He simply touched Procter's sword, then touched his own tomahawk, and said, "You are Procter. I am Tecumseh."

Procter understood that Tecumseh meant to fight him, hand to hand. Immediately, he gave orders that the food given to the native people and the British was to be the same.

Now Procter was afraid that the Native Americans would desert him. He heard that the British had lost a battle on Lake Erie. It was the most important battle of the war. But he did not dare tell Tecumseh the truth about the battle. And at the same time, Procter secretly began making plans to retreat.

But Tecumseh knew Procter's plans. He assembled his warriors on the Fort Malden parade ground and, looking straight at Procter, he said:

"You always told us to remain here and take care of our lands. It made our hearts glad to hear you say that was your wish. . . . You always told us that you would never draw your foot off British ground. But now we see that you are pulling back . . . We must compare your conduct to a fat animal that carries its tail on its back, but when frightened, drops it between its legs and runs."

Tecumseh saw Procter's face turn pale.

"Listen!" Tecumseh continued. "You have the arms and ammunition which our great father sent for his red children. If you have an idea of going away, give them to us, and you may go. . . . We will never give up."

Badly frightened, Procter made for his quarters. Now he feared Tecumseh and his loyal warriors almost as much as he feared the Americans.

Tecumseh was not alone in wanting to defend the fort. The British soldiers wanted to fight for their fort — not retreat.

Procter felt his soldiers' anger rise toward him. He knew Tecumseh hated him. Finally, Procter said he would not retreat altogether; he would make a stand near the Thames River.

One night, while Tecumseh was dining with the officers, a messenger came in with the news that a huge American fleet was sailing up the Detroit River.

Tecumseh rose, put his hands on the pistols General Brock had given him, and said to Procter:

> "We must go meet the enemy and prevent them from coming here. We must not retreat. If you take us from this place you will lead us to the mercy of the [Americans]. I am tired of it all. Every word you say blows to nothing, like the smoke from our pipes. You are like the crawfish that does not know how to walk straight ahead!"

Procter assembled his men and at once began his move to the Thames River.

Tecumseh assembled his army of approximately five hundred Shawnee warriors and followed the British. Together, their army numbered over a thousand.

On October 4, Tecumseh learned that General Harrison was approaching the Thames River with a large force.

The night was chilly. Tecumseh sat with his warriors around the fire. Suddenly, he looked up and said, "Brother warriors, we are about to enter an engagement from which I shall not return. My body will remain on the field of battle."

Both sides spent the next morning planning the battle that was to come.

Tecumseh told his own warriors to "be brave, stand firm, and shoot straight."

In anticipation of a good fight, Tecumseh's spirits rose. Then he walked up to General Procter and said in a friendly voice, "Have a big heart. Tell your young men to be firm and all will be well."

At four o'clock in the afternoon, the British and the Native Americans heard the clear notes of the American bugles sounding through the woods.

Then the Americans charged.

Procter fled. But most of his soldiers and all of the Shawnee warriors remained to fight. And while the gunfire burst all around them in the woods, Tecumseh's voice could be heard, urging his men forward to attack.

He was wounded again and again. Still, he battled on.

But before the battle was over, Tecumseh was dead.

✕✕✕

In the years that followed, the Indian Nations grew smaller and smaller. Soon towns stood where hunting grounds had been.

But it would take more than death to erase the memory of Tecumseh. The *Indiana Sentinel* of December 2, 1820 said:

> "Tecumseh was a great man. He was truly great —
> and his greatness was his own, unassisted by
> science or the aids of education. As a statesman,
> a warrior, and a patriot, we shall not look upon his
> like again."

COCHISE

Cochise.
A portrait
based on
descriptions
of the Apache
chief.

1
DAYS OF PEACE

ochise was at peace.

The most powerful Apache chief was at peace with the white man. His warriors had not fought the white men in five years.

In 1860, signs of peace were everywhere in Cochise's village. The *wickiups*, the round houses covered with thatch and deerskin, were sturdy and well built. If this were wartime, the wickiups would be made in a much simpler, cruder way so that the tribe could break up camp and be gone in a matter of minutes.

There were many Apache tribes in the land that is now Arizona. Cochise's tribe was called the Chiricahua Apaches, and though they were the smallest tribe, they were the most powerful of them all.

At this time Cochise was about fifty years old, yet he had the strength and the look of a younger man. He stood almost six feet tall — taller than any of his warriors. He

Apache wickiup, 1903.

had the straight, powerful body of a fighting man and the deep, intelligent eyes of a thinking man.

He was born around 1810. Early in life, he began to train for the hunt and the battle.

He learned how to make weapons, how to use them with speed and accuracy, and how to dodge them just as skillfully.

He learned to be like a rock — silent and still for hours; to make no sound when wounded, no sound as he attacked.

He learned to be like a deer — to run for miles, for hours over hot, sandy desert and rough mountain places without stopping for rest, food, or drink.

Heat, cold, hunger, thirst — all these he knew how to live with. But even then, he was not a warrior.

Like every young boy of his tribe, he had to show that he could live alone. For two weeks, alone in the deserts and mountains, he ate and drank only what he could find in the barren land.

Yet even then, he was not a warrior. Four times he had to go to battle — not to fight, but to run errands for the fighting warriors.

After that, and only then, could an Apache boy call himself a warrior.

Now, as Cochise watched the children of his tribe playing their games of war, he was glad that soon new warriors would add strength to his small tribe.

Not that five or six warriors — or even fifty or sixty! — would make much difference, Cochise thought, *compared to the number of white men who have come to our land.*

How can I even number them? he wondered. It would be like trying to count drops of rain or grains of desert sand. There seemed to be no end to the white man.

No wonder it seemed this way to Cochise. For hundreds of years, the Apache tribes had roamed these deserts, these mountains, these canyons and forests. Then came the Mexicans. The Apaches were constantly at war with them, but in the end they were able to keep the Mexicans off Apache land.

But then from the East came the Americans. These

deserts, these mountains, these canyons and forests, they said, were now theirs.

Cochise and his people did not know that the United States, only seventy-two years old in 1848, was involved in a grim war with Mexico. The Apaches did not know that after the war, and after the purchase of land from Mexico, there was a new boundary between the United States and Mexico. Nearly all the Apache land was on the United States side of the boundary, in what is now Arizona and New Mexico.

In the land lived fifty thousand Native Americans of various tribes, among them, the Apache tribes. Until 1853, there had been only five thousand white men.

Now the white men poured into Apache country.

Settlers came. They built cattle ranches and grazed their cattle on Apache land.

Miners came. They dug into the native peoples' land for gold and silver. Then, when the Apaches tried to protect their land, soldiers came. The soldiers built forts to protect the ranchers and miners.

Settlers, miners, soldiers — all invaders on Apache land.

※ ※ ※

At first the Apaches had tried to fight the American citizens as they had the Mexicans. But the Americans had deadly weapons and it seemed there was no end to the number of men who fired them.

In two years, it was alarming how many Apaches were killed.

As his people mourned the fallen warriors, Cochise would spend long hours thinking sadly that his tribe might soon become only a name lost to memory.

We cannot fight them or destroy them, he thought. *They grow stronger while we grow weaker.*

Cochise came to a very important decision. He would make peace with the white man. Only in that way could his tribe survive.

Of all the many Apache tribes, not one was at peace with the white men. To think of peace was unheard of.

The miner rinsed away soil from his pan.
"Gold! We're rich, boys!"

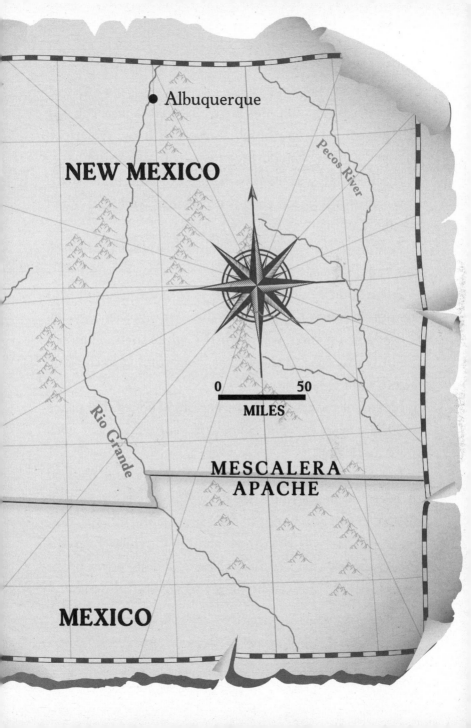

Could Cochise possibly convince the white men that his offer of peace was sincere?

At Fort Buchanan, not far from what is now the city of Tucson, Arizona, Cochise met with an American colonel. Colonel Enoch Steen was the officer in charge of the fort. He was an intelligent man who understood how important peace with the Apaches could be. Steen trusted Cochise and peace was made.

And now, for five years, Cochise saw to it that peace was kept.

All around Cochise's tribe — across the mountains to the north, down the valley to the east — other Apache tribes kept up their war with the white men. They felt the only way to stop the whites from coming to the land was to fight them.

Not all of the Chiricahua warriors believed that peace was the way to survive. Some still yearned for war with the Americans.

But every warrior knew that Cochise had pledged to keep his peace and that he would never break that pledge. Truth and honor had a value among all Apaches, but in no man was it stronger than in Cochise. Even his enemies knew that Cochise never told a lie, never broke a promise, and showed no mercy to anyone who did.

2

UNDER THE WHITE FLAG

n January 1861, trouble came to Cochise's people. It began when a little boy named Felix Ward was kidnapped. The kidnapping took place not far from the village where the Chiricahua Apaches lived.

Felix's mother was a Mexican woman who had been captured by a northern tribe called the Pinal Apaches. Felix's father was a Pinal Apache who died when Felix Ward was still a baby. After the death of her husband, Felix's mother took her child and ran away from the Pinal Apaches.

She came to a ranch owned by John Ward, a white man, and began keeping house for him. Ward adopted her son, but the Pinal Apaches said that Felix was an Apache. They vowed to get him back.

John Ward was not at home on that fateful day the Pinal Apaches came to his ranch. One of them snatched up Felix and galloped off. The others drove off Ward's cattle and horses. The Pinal Apaches lived to the west of Ward's ranch. But cleverly, they rode first to the east, then turned west and headed home.

When Ward discovered the boy was missing, he swore revenge. He followed the tracks of the horses and cattle and saw that they led eastward — in the direction of the Chiricahua village. Ward immediately assumed that it was Cochise and the Chiricahua Apaches who had kidnapped Felix.

John Ward was stubborn and quick-tempered. It was said that once he made his mind up about anything, he never changed it. It was known, too, how he hated the native people.

He galloped to Fort Buchanan, twelve miles away. Unfortunately, Colonel Steen was no longer in command of the fort there. Ward told the new commander, Lieutenant Colonel Pitcairn Morrison, what had happened. He supposedly singled out the Chiricahua Apaches, claiming they had kidnapped Felix and stolen his cattle.

Morrison was surprised. Was Ward sure that the Chiricahua Apaches had kidnapped the boy? Didn't Ward know that Cochise had kept peace faithfully?

It was impossible to reason with Ward. The idea that there could be peace and honor with the Native Americans was plain nonsense to him. To him, they were savages.

He demanded that Morrison act fast.

✳ ✳ ✳

Perhaps the whole kidnapping incident might have soon been forgotten had it not been for a young second lieutenant. History might have told a different story if Lieutenant George Bascom had not come one day to Fort Buchanan.

Lieutenant Bascom was young and inexperienced. Just out of the United States Military Academy, he had never been in battle. He didn't know anything about the Apache Indians or their ways — indeed, he had never even seen a Native American.

Bascom was sent out to find the kidnapped child and bring him and the stolen cattle back to John Ward. Under no uncertain orders, Bascom was to get the boy back. Even though Colonel Morrison explained to Lieutenant Bascom that Cochise and his tribe had been at peace with the Americans for five years, Bascom concluded that Cochise and the Chiricahua Apaches had taken Felix.

Morrison gave Bascom fifty-four mounted men and an interpreter who spoke Apache. John Ward insisted on going with him.

It was Bascom's first command. He knew nothing about the native people except what he had heard. And what he heard were only tales of ignorance and cruelty.

Bascom remained convinced that Cochise had taken Ward's boy.

After four days of riding through desert and mountains and canyons, they came to the mail station at Apache Pass. Apache Pass was an important stop on the mail route that linked the East to the West. Directly above, in the mountains, lay Cochise's village.

It was clear at a glance that this was a peaceful place. Apache children were playing happily. Some of the Chiricahua Apaches were cutting wood and hay for the people at the mail station. And close to the mail station were the huts in which some of the Apaches lived. There were no soldiers.

A Butterfield stagecoach. One of these specially built coaches was the first to carry mail through Apache country.

Lieutenant Bascom sent word to Cochise that he wanted to meet with him.

His arrival was no surprise to Cochise. For some time, his scouts had been following every step of Bascom's approach.

Cochise came down the mountain. With him came his wife and son, his brother, and two nephews. No one was armed. Cochise had only his hunting knife that he used every day.

Bascom had put up his tent some distance from the station. Cochise saw soldiers standing around the tent, but he led his people inside. The Apaches sat on the ground and waited in silence.

Those who knew Apache ways understood that the silence was considered good manners. Silence let the other person get used to a new presence, gave them time to think.

Bascom knew little about Apache ways. The young lieutenant began to speak of the raid on Ward's ranch, of the stolen horses and cattle, of the kidnapped boy.

When the words were translated, Cochise wondered what they had to do with him or his tribe.

It was then that Bascom accused Cochise of having stolen the boy and the cattle. He demanded that they be returned at once.

Cochise sat stunned. He held back his anger and for a long while he was silent, trying to stay calm.

He would explain the situation to this young man and he must do it as carefully as he would explain it to a child. Slowly, Cochise explained that for more than five years his people had been at peace and had not killed any white man or taken anything that belonged to the white man. Instead, they had helped the wagons and mail coaches pass safely through the land. They had even killed native people from other tribes who attacked the white travelers, in order to keep this peace.

Bascom looked at Ward. Ward insisted Cochise was lying, that he had taken the boy and the cattle.

Cochise fought to control his rage. He told Bascom that he knew nothing about the boy or the cattle. He offered to help find them and suggested that one of the warring tribes in the region — the Pinal Apaches, the Coyotero Apaches, or the White Mountain Apaches — may have been involved.

Bascom refused the offer of help and accused Cochise of lying. He told Cochise that he would hold him and his warriors hostage until the boy and the cattle were returned. Then he made a move to take Cochise and his warriors prisoner.

A wild cry filled the tent. A knife glittered. It is said that Cochise jumped to his feet and was across the tent in an instant. "Follow me!" he cried to his people. In seconds, he slashed open the canvas wall with his knife and, leaping through the tent, he began to run.

Cochise had taken the guards completely by surprise. When they realized what had happened, they began to shoot. Cochise dashed up the steep hill.

One of his brother's sons was stabbed in the stomach with a bayonet. His wife, brother, and nephews — and Cochise's son — were seized.

Only Cochise escaped.

3

COCHISE'S PLEDGE

ochise made his way back to the hills, where his warriors were waiting. Together, they rode down to the station.

His plan was to take as captives the three white men who were at the station. He would hold them only long enough to ask for an exchange of prisoners. As soon as he got his family back, the three white men would be set free.

But it was not to be that simple.

It was easy enough to capture the three men at the station. They had always been friendly with Cochise and his people. They had not yet heard what had taken place inside Bascom's tent.

So they walked out, unarmed, to greet the Apaches. Cochise's men seized them immediately. Two of the men struggled free and ran toward the stone wall behind the station. Before Cochise could stop him, an Apache warrior fired and one of the white men fell dead.

Just at that moment, some of Lieutenant Bascom's men were on their way back to the station. They heard the shooting.

One of the soldiers saw a man climbing over the stone wall. He fired — not at a Native American as he supposed, but at one of the escaping white men.

Meanwhile, the Chiricahua Apaches took their one remaining captive back to their mountain fortress.

Immediately, Cochise ordered his men to ride to

An Apache warrior attacking a covered wagon. A painting by Frederic Remington. The artist lived with cowboys and Native Americans, and his paintings capture the action of the Wild West.

Apache Pass. He asked that they stop stagecoaches and wagon trains from going through. He also asked them to bring him white prisoners.

Before the day was done his men returned with three captured white men.

The next morning, Cochise and many warriors rode out of the forest. With them was the prisoner they had captured at the station, a man called James Wallace. Cochise's plan was to have this man help explain to Bascom what Cochise wanted — an exchange of prisoners.

Wallace's presence gained the soldiers' attention. A stick was placed in the ground with a note attached to it. Cochise had instructed Wallace to write the following message: "Treat my people well and I will do the same by yours, of whom I have four."

This is when Bascom found out that Cochise was holding three more white men and that he would trade the four of them for the Apache prisoners.

Bascom's voice was cool. "Tell him he'll get his Apaches when we get the Ward boy and the cattle." The young second lieutenant walked back to the station without another word.

This impossible request again! How could Cochise return what he had not taken?

Meanwhile, in the dark storeroom of the station, Cochise's family huddled together. Cochise's wife tried to comfort her young son. The boy tried to act like a man. Cochise's nephew was slowly recovering from the bayonet wound he had received.

Cochise's warriors clamored for war. Cochise wondered how much longer he could hold them back.

But he was determined to try to save the peace — at least once more.

Once more Cochise and his warriors came down from the mountain, but this time more than a hundred warriors lined the ridge. Their faces were streaked with war paint and each man held a weapon. Cochise sat tall and erect on his war pony, wearing in his headband the eagle plumes of warfare.

Cochise did not need to have any words translated. He saw Bascom's stubborn face, saw hope dying in Wallace's eyes.

He gave an order. The Chiricahua Apaches rode back into the hills with their captives. They killed the four white men and left their bodies there as a message to Bascom and his men.

Later the soldiers found the bodies. They rode back at once to the depot. In retaliation, they hanged the male Apache hostages — Cochise's brother and nephews. They spared and later released Cochise's wife and son.

When scouts brought Cochise the news, he mounted

his swiftest pony and rode down the mountain. He saw, hanging from a tree, the bodies of his relatives along with three other Coyoteros Apaches that had been captured. He forced himself to gaze at the bodies for a long, long time. Then he cut them down and brought them back to his village.

The wives of his brother and his nephews lay down and beat the earth. They painted the dead men's faces and dressed them in their finest clothes so that they would look their best for the long journey to the gods. Then they burned their wickiups and killed their horses and cattle. Everything the dead men had owned was thrown into the flames.

They covered their heads and the heads of their children with black shawls and went far from the village to mourn.

For twenty days, Cochise mourned with them.

On the twenty-first day, a fire was lighted.

The medicine man threw powder into the fire. Great clouds of black smoke spiraled upward. Cochise raised his arms and lifted his face to the sky.

It is said Cochise then pledged a war to the end with the white men.

For the first time in five years, the war cries of Cochise's tribe rang through the canyons and echoed in the mountains.

Felix Ward. Raised to adulthood by the Pinal Apaches who had kidnapped him as a child, Felix later became a scout, guide, and interpreter for the U.S. Army. He went by the name of Mickey Free.

4

WAR!

ieutenant Bascom had unleashed a war of fury.

Cochise knew that the enemy forces were far greater than the Apaches'. It was as if a single tree tried to fight a forest. He knew that the different Apache tribes must join together to fight their enemy.

And so, for the first time in many years, Apache tribes stopped warring among themselves. Apache war chiefs from near and far now gathered in Cochise's stronghold.

One of the older chiefs was Cochise's father-in-law, Mangas Coloradas. The Americans called him Red Sleeves. Seventy-one-year-old Mangas had been fighting for many years, ever since some miners tied him up and beat him — as a warning to stay away from their camp.

The Apache war chiefs planned their strategy well. As a single army, under Cochise, the Apache Nation rode to battle.

From the canyons, the mountains, and the deserts of the great Southwest, their war cries rang out.

From a dozen different places, they made their lightning attacks. Ranches and villages were burned and settlers driven from their homes. Mines were destroyed and miners fled for their lives. No white man dared travel through Apache Pass, and the stage line was abandoned.

Cochise had been at war only two months when two thousand miles away — at Fort Sumter in South Carolina — the burst of a cannon marked the start of the American Civil War. The year was 1861.

Cochise had no way of knowing about this war that threatened to tear the United States apart, but he soon felt its influence. The army needed men. Soldiers were ordered to leave their southwestern posts and to burn their forts behind them.

Scouts hurried to tell Cochise that the forts were in flames and the soldiers were fleeing. Some Apaches thought this was a sign of their victory. Cochise was wise enough to know otherwise.

They had not yet done battle with the soldiers and had not attacked their forts. Their leaving could have nothing to do with the Apaches.

Now, with the soldiers gone, the Apache raids reached farther and farther — even to the booming town of Tucson. Tucson had been one of the most rapidly growing towns in the Southwest. Now the settlers there fled to

California, and soon there were only two hundred people left.

In 1865, the Civil War was over but the Apache Wars went on — wars that Cochise did not choose or want.

Soon after the Civil War, soldiers returned to the Southwest. They had their orders from the United States government. The orders were to kill Apache men and take Apache women and children prisoners. Within a year, two thousand Apache women and children had been captured. In that same year — 1866 — one county in the Arizona Territory was still offering $250 for every Apache scalp brought in.

❊ ❊ ❊

It was not always easy for the soldiers to find the Apaches. Under Cochise's command, the Apaches were an army of ghosts. They struck — they vanished — they struck again.

They rode their war ponies with speed. They could ride bareback a hundred miles in one day, on narrow mountain and desert trails known only to them. The soldiers had to stay on the main road. They were slowed down by the heavy packs of equipment their mules carried.

The Apaches rode in silence, using as signals the bark of the fox, the call of the bird, and the cry of the coyote. Alternately, the clink of the soldiers' spurs and their rifle-shot signals made their whereabouts known.

The Apaches could get food and drink from the cactus and could ride for many hours without rest. The soldiers had to stop often and make camp.

The U.S. government spent millions of dollars and sent streams of soldiers to wipe out the Apaches. But Cochise — sometimes with fewer than two hundred warriors — defeated the U.S. Army soldiers again and again.

5

A MAN TO TRUST

homas Jonathan Jeffords had done many daring things in his thirty years of life. He had been captain of a riverboat on the Mississippi River, prospected for gold in Indian country, and scouted for the government during the Civil War.

Now in Tucson, he held an almost impossible job. He had to see that the mail got through Apache country. He hired the most reckless riders, armed them with the best rifles, mounted them on the fastest horses, and paid them more money than anyone had before. But rider after rider was killed. In fifteen months, Jeffords lost twenty-two men.

It seemed hopeless to try to get the mail through.

But Thomas Jeffords had a plan.

He would seek out Cochise and make a private peace with him. He had heard from many men that for seven years no white man had seen Cochise and lived to tell of it. But he remembered hearing that Cochise was an honest and brave man who admired honesty and bravery in others.

Jeffords worked for months to learn Apache language and Apache ways. He learned to separate the lies from the truth told about Cochise. Then he asked a friendly Apache boy living near Tucson to show him the way to Cochise's camp. The boy was startled, but he agreed to help. Without telling anyone else, the two set out.

After riding some distance, the boy said he must turn back. It was then unsafe for Apaches to travel with whites beyond that point.

The boy turned back to Tucson, and Jeffords was alone in Apache country — alone with the silence of the land, alone with the trees and the rocks, where perhaps right at that moment an Apache was hiding with a rifle in his hand.

Jeffords built small fires and sent up smoke signals that he knew could be seen for many miles. The smoke signals said he traveled alone and in peace. Jeffords knew his only hope in reaching Cochise alive was to travel openly and boldly, to arouse Cochise's curiosity and not to show fear.

Cochise was indeed curious. He gave orders to his warriors not to harm the white man, but to watch him carefully.

Thomas Jeffords riding into Chiricahua territory.

For hours, Jeffords traveled in the rough, mountainous country. Apache eyes watched his every move.

Then suddenly, he was in Cochise's camp, surrounded by Apaches. Behind the circle of Apaches, Jeffords saw a tall, older man and knew this was Cochise.

Thomas Jeffords got off his horse as calmly as he could. He knew that if he showed fear, all would be lost. He handed his weapons — rifle, knife, revolver — to an Indian woman, then he said in perfect Apache, "Hold these for me until I leave."

He walked up to Cochise and stood silently before him, as was the Apache way. His heart was pounding, but he kept his face calm. After a long while, Jeffords began by saying that he had no wish to be at war with Cochise. He told Cochise why he had come and what he wanted.

For a long time Cochise looked at this white man, with his strange red beard and his honest eyes. Then he motioned Jeffords to follow him to his wickiup.

The two men talked long into the night. They talked about many things. Jeffords told Cochise about his country, his president, why his people were coming now to Apache country, and why it was important for the United States to have Apache Pass open, so that settlers could travel westward. He told Cochise about the mail riders who had been killed though they came not to make war but to carry the mail through.

Cochise spoke of the years in which Apache, too, had been at peace but had been killed, and how he had kept the white men safe from other tribes.

Cochise told Jeffords many stories of how the white men betrayed the Apaches. Jeffords did not try to make excuses for the white men's behavior. Cochise respected him even more for this.

Cochise discovered that he liked this white man and even felt he could trust him. Jeffords's admiration for the great chief also grew with every passing hour.

The following day, Cochise said, "Your riders can pass safely through these mountains. And you, *Taglito*, are my friend and will always be welcomed here."

Jeffords smiled at the Apache word for "red beard." Taglito. He liked the name.

Cochise kept his word as Jeffords knew he would. Though the war went on and the white men and the Apaches continued to fight, Jeffords's riders carried the mail safely through Apache Pass.

In the months that followed, Jeffords came often to Cochise's camp, and the friendship between the two men grew stronger.

They talked of war and they talked of peace. No longer were there four thousand Apache warriors united in fighting the enemy. By now the greater part of the Apache Nation had been defeated in battle and those who survived had been sent to live on reservations.

In Cochise's band there were fewer than three hundred people. But Cochise did not surrender. He had been told what had happened to the Apache tribes that had put down their arms and now lived on reservations. Soldiers guarded them day and night. The white men in charge of the native people's welfare took the food that was meant for the native people.

Cochise had also heard about what had happened to the Aravaipa Apache Nation. They had gone to Camp Grant near Tucson, wishing to make peace with the army. The army had put them up in huts overnight. Before dawn, a mob from Tucson attacked them. They went from hut to hut, clubbing the sleeping Aravaipa Apaches to death.

Americans across the nation were horrified by the crime. President Grant wrote to the governor, describing the event as "purely murder." One hundred Americans, Mexicans, and Papago Indians, deadly enemies of the Apaches, were charged with the murders. The jury, however, declared them not guilty.

The massacre at Camp Grant had made many more Americans aware of the cruelty with which the Native Americans were being treated. President Grant was now more anxious than ever to end the Apache Wars. In ten years, the wars had cost the U.S. government one thousand lives and forty million dollars.

Now the government spoke of a policy of kindness and firmness and peace. But it was not enough for President Grant to speak of such a policy. He had to convince Cochise that he meant it.

In the fall of 1871, President Grant sent a special soldier to Arizona, one whom he believed could make peace with Cochise.

That man was General Oliver Otis Howard. Many men called him "the Christian General." He kept his Bible with him always and he read from it every day. With his flowing hair and beard, some thought he looked as if he might have stepped out of the Bible.

As soon as General Howard arrived in Arizona, he sought out Jeffords, the one man, he had been told, who

General Oliver Otis Howard, called "the Christian General."

could lead him to Cochise. Howard told Jeffords that President Grant had given him full powers to make any settlement with Cochise that he thought was right. Jeffords agreed to take Howard to meet Cochise, but asked that Howard come without soldiers. Howard agreed.

Jeffords felt a hope he had not experienced in years, a hope that this man might very well be the one to end eleven terrible years of war.

The journey to Cochise's mountains took many days. On the way, General Howard asked many questions. Jeffords told the general that Cochise was an honorable man and that if he gave his word he would keep it. Jeffords spoke of Cochise's dignity and honesty and how his people followed him as they would a king. He said that few white men had tried to understand him and that if only Lieutenant Bascom had, this war may not have started in the first place.

⁕ ⁕ ⁕

Several Chiricahua Apaches joined Howard and his men on their way. One day they passed through a settlement of gold miners. The miners blocked their path, shouting, "Apache murderers! Kill 'em!" It has been said that General Howard quickly stepped between the miners and the Chiricahua Apaches. In a calm, firm voice, he said, "If any killing is done, you must kill me first." The crowd fell back and Howard led his party on.

6

PEACE WITH HONOR

inally, General Howard and the Chiricahua Apaches reached Cochise's camp.

Cochise met General Howard with great dignity. Jeffords explained to Cochise why the general had come. Cochise trusted Jeffords, and so was willing to at least hear what Howard had come to say.

Cochise and Howard talked and Jeffords translated. Cochise told about the peace he had made long ago and how he had protected the travelers in Apache Pass.

He told how he had promised peace and how he had kept his promise. Then he told the story of Lieutenant Bascom's treachery.

When his story was told, he asked the general how long he would stay. Howard said he would stay as long as it would take to make peace. He also offered to move Cochise's people to good land on the Rio Grande River.

Cochise did not want to move his people. He told Howard that this land was their home. Howard listened to Cochise. He suggested creating a reservation for Cochise and his people right there on their same land.

Cochise took Howard to a high ridge that overlooked the land. The general could see why Cochise and his people could not leave the land — its mountains, forests, streams, and canyons. The setting sun warmed the clay cliff walls, deepened the greens of the forests, and tinted the mountain ranges purple.

In the days that followed, Cochise named his terms. His people must be allowed to keep their weapons. They were not a conquered nation and they were not surrendering. They were making peace as free men. And they did not want any thieving agents overseeing their lives. He said that if a government agent would have to be present, then the only agent he would accept would be Jeffords.

Jeffords did not necessarily want to be a Native American agent. Howard could tell, however, that the only way for there to be peace between the Apaches and the whites would be for Jeffords to fill that post.

Jeffords looked at his Apache friend and thought how important this peace would be.

He sighed and said at last, "I will take the job."

Cochise agreed to call his people to a council of peace. He said that it would be many days before they could all come together, for many were out on hunts and raids.

While waiting for the warriors to return, General Howard and Cochise talked often, and Howard's admiration for Cochise grew every day. Often he thought, *The United States could use more men like Cochise, with his honor and his military genius.*

Chiricahua Apache chief Naiche (son of Cochise) with his wife.

The general kept a diary of his days in Cochise's mountains, and while he wrote, the children gathered around him. Howard taught Cochise's youngest son how to write his name in English. Sometimes the general would rest on a blanket out of doors and the children would lie down next to him.

Their raids and hunts over, Cochise's warriors slowly drifted back into the camp. When they had all gathered, Cochise took them to the council grounds and the white men were asked to stay behind until they were called for.

For five days, Jeffords and Howard waited.

When they were finally asked to join the council, Howard thought he had never before seen such an impressive sight. The warriors were seated in a circle and around them, in a larger circle, were the women. Cochise stood in the center, his face lifted to the sky.

Cochise told Jeffords and Howard that he and his people would follow the terms of their peace agreement from this day forward. Several Apaches, however, had not been in agreement, and Cochise let Jeffords and Howard know that those particular Apaches would no longer be welcome there.

And as long as both Cochise and Jeffords lived, peace was kept between the Americans and the Chiricahua Apaches.

Cochise died in 1874. He did not live to see the final fate of his people. For the promise made by Howard was later broken and they were driven out of their mountain home and moved to a distant reservation.

High in the Arizona mountains, where the Chiricahua Apaches had lived, there is a mountain peak that is called Cochise Stronghold.

Somewhere near this mountain peak, Cochise is buried. The only white man who knew exactly where was Thomas Jeffords. And he kept the secret.